Riviera Maya

TRAVEL

GUIDE

2023

An Itinerary Guide to Riviera Maya's
Exploration, Cuisine, Top Hidden gems and
more in 2023

Dan C. Bernardi

Table of Contents

INTRODUCTION

1.1 About the Riviera Maya

The Riviera Maya, a tropical paradise that combines a rich history, magnificent natural beauty, and contemporary comfort, is located on the Yucatán Peninsula in Mexico. This section of the Caribbean coast is well-known for its gorgeous white sand beaches, turquoise oceans, and a variety of attractions that make it a popular travel destination for people all over the world.

The length of the Riviera Maya, from Tulum in the south to Cancun in the north, is around 120 miles. It bears the name of the legendary Mayan civilisation, which flourished here in antiquity and left behind some amazing archaeological monuments and cultural practices. The ruins of Tulum and Cobá, which offer interesting glimpses into the past, are accessible to visitors to this region. In addition, the Riviera Maya is home to the renowned Chichen Itza, one of the

New Seven Wonders of the World and a reminder of the area's lengthy past.

This area is a sanctuary for outdoor enthusiasts as well as being significant historically. The Riviera Maya offers a variety of chances for hiking, snorkeling, scuba diving, and other adventurous activities thanks to its lush jungles, underground cenotes, and bright coral reefs.

1.2 How to Use This Guide

Your key to discovering the Riviera Maya's riches is this travel guide. Our book is intended to give you in-depth information, insider insights, and practical guidance to make your trip pleasurable and memorable, whether you're a first-time visitor or returning to explore more of this breathtaking location.

Navigation: The guide is divided into several sections, each of which focuses on a different element of your trip to Riviera Maya. It's simple to navigate to the area of the website that most appeals to you, whether it's the section on itinerary planning, cultural heritage exploration, or where to eat well.

Recommendations: In order to give you chosen suggestions for lodging, activities, food, and more, we've taken the time to filter through a myriad of possibilities. Our aim is to assist you in making decisions that are in line with your tastes and financial constraints.

Insider Information: We've gathered recommendations from seasoned travelers and local experts to provide you access to useful information that only locals would be able to offer.

1.3 Travel Tips and Safety Information

Your health and safety are of utmost significance as you tour the Riviera Maya. Despite the fact that it's a generally safe and inviting place, it's important to be aware of certain important travel advice and safety information.

Health and Hygiene: Because the tropical environment can be harsh, it's advised to drink enough of water, use sunscreen, and avoid insect bites. Make sure your vaccines are current and have any essential prescriptions. Keep up with regional health laws, particularly in light of the current global health situation.

Local Laws and Customs: It's important to respect regional traditions and customs. Even though the Riviera Maya is a tourist-friendly area, it is important to wear modest clothing when visiting sacred or historical locations. Avoid making public shows of affection, which some cultures may find rude.

Safety: Although the Riviera Maya is well regarded for its safety, it is advisable to exercise caution wherever you go. Keep an eye on your possessions, refrain from flaunting expensive items in public, and store valuables and critical papers in hotel safes. Keep to well-lit places and reliable transportation when touring after dark.

Money & Finances: Although U.S. dollars are generally accepted in tourist areas, the native currency is the Mexican Peso (MXN). Carrying some pesos is advisable for minor purchases and locations that might not take foreign currencies. There are several ATMs where you may exchange currencies, but beware of potential fees.

Communication: The majority of tourist regions speak English, however knowing a few fundamental Spanish words might be useful and well-liked by locals. Make sure you have a functioning cell phone or a local SIM card so you can use navigation apps and keep connected. 911 is the local emergency number, and 060 is the number for tourist assistance.

As you learn more about the Riviera Maya, you can find more detailed information in this guide regarding safety, particular health considerations, and local laws. Our goal is to arm you with the information you need to enjoy a wonderful and secure trip to this alluring location. The Riviera Maya guarantees an exploration and adventure-filled voyage, whether you're here for the historical wonders, the breathtaking beaches, or the vibrant culture.

It's time to start your voyage of discovery in this captivating region of the world now that you have a firm grasp on what the Riviera Maya has to offer and how to use this guide. Have fun on your trip to the Riviera Maya!

GETTING TO THE RIVIERA MAYA

Planning your trip to this magical location is the next step after being seduced by the Riviera Maya's beauty and charm. This section will discuss several modes of transportation as well as the crucial visa and entry criteria you should be aware of before starting your adventure.

2.1 Transportation Options

Due to its excellent connectivity, the Riviera Maya is accessible from many locations throughout the globe. Your location and personal preferences will determine the mode of transportation you choose. The most popular ways to travel to the Riviera Maya are listed below:

Air travel: Flying into Cancun International Airport (CUN) is the most popular method of getting to the Riviera Maya. Many international airlines offer direct flights to this important airport from a variety of places in the United States, Canada, Europe, and other parts of the world. You'll be in a good place to explore the Riviera Maya when you get there.

Ground Transportation: You can choose ground transportation if you're already in Mexico or if you'd want to take a beautiful road trip. From adjacent cities and regions, one can get to the region by automobile or bus. If you intend to travel outside of your resort or hotel, it is advised that you rent a car. In general, the road system is well-kept and simple to use.

Cruise: Traveling to the Riviera Maya by cruise ship is another wonderful option. There are several cruise lines that provide itineraries with stops in the area. You can take day trips to see the nearby sights when your cruise docks, guaranteeing a wonderful experience.

Public Transportation: Within the Riviera Maya, there is a network of buses that you can use to get from town to town and attraction to attraction. Although they are a less expensive choice, they might not be the most practical for those with a lot of luggage or strict schedules.

2.2 Visa and Entry Requirements

You must be informed of the visa and entry regulations in order to enter the Riviera Maya without incident. These specifications change based on your nationality, the reason for your trip, and how long you plan to remain.

Tourist Visa: For brief stays in Mexico (less than 180 days), the majority of visitors do not need a visa. Tourist visas are not required for entry into Mexico for citizens of other nations. The particular requirements, however, are subject to change, therefore it is imperative to confirm with the local Mexican consulate or embassy before your travel. Please make sure your passport is valid for at least six more months beyond the day you intend to depart.

A tourist card (Forma Migratoria Mltiple, FMM) will be given to you when you arrive at Cancun International Airport. With this card, you are permitted a 180-day tourist stay in Mexico. During your stay, keep it with you, and give it back when you go. You might occasionally need to fork over money to use the FMM.

Visitor with Business Purposes: If you intend to go to the Riviera Maya for professional reasons, such as to conduct business meetings or attend a conference, you might need to apply for a business visa. For up-to-date information on requirements, it is advised to get in touch with the Mexican embassy or consulate in your place of residence.

Work or Study: Prior to your arrival, you must secure the necessary visa and permit if you plan to work or study in Mexico. It is advised to start the application process well in advance because getting a work or study visa might be more difficult and time-consuming.

Customs Declaration: You must abide by certain customs laws in Mexico. Make sure you fill out a customs declaration form when you arrive and list any valuables you are bringing. Items that are not declared may be fined or taken.

COVID-19 criteria: As COVID-19-related admission criteria, such as testing or vaccination, may change, please stay up to date on any updates. Check the rules for traveling during the pandemic with your airline, the Mexican government, and your own nation.

In conclusion, you should carefully plan your trip to the Riviera Maya and be aware of your options for getting there as well as the regulations for admittance. You can go off on your excursion with confidence and readiness to enjoy the wonders of this remarkable location if you have the necessary documents in your possession. The accommodation alternatives for a relaxing and enjoyable stay in the Riviera Maya are covered in the next section of this guide.

ACCOMMODATION

Your choice of where to sleep plays a big role in how you experience Riviera Maya. The area has a wide variety of lodging choices to suit any traveler's needs and budget. There is something for everyone, from opulent beachfront resorts to welcoming vacation rentals and immersive eco-lodges.

3.1 Hotels and Resorts

There are several hotels and resorts in the Riviera Maya, from luxurious all-inclusive mega-resorts to boutique hotels that provide a more individualized experience. Here's a detailed look at what to anticipate:

All-inclusive resorts are a popular option if you're looking for convenience and luxury. These places often provide unlimited food, beverages, and entertainment, letting you unwind without being concerned about additional costs. Many of the Riviera Maya's all-inclusive resorts are located on immaculate beaches, making it simple to access the sand and water. Spa services, entertainment, water sports, and excellent cuisine are available as amenities.

Boutique hotels are a great choice for tourists looking for a more personal and distinctive stay. A more individualized and romantic environment is produced by the unusual architecture and décor of these modest residences. You'll get specialized care and an opportunity to fully experience the culture.

Resorts that cater to families: If you're vacationing with kids, the Riviera Maya has resorts that do just that. These facilities frequently provide kid-friendly amenities including kiddie pools and clubs as well as family-friendly activities. Both parents and children can enjoy their holiday in a secure and enjoyable setting thanks to them.

Adults-Only Resorts: If you're looking for a tranquil getaway, think about going to an adults-only hotel. These homes are made to offer a peaceful environment, perfect for couples and people seeking romance and leisure. Enjoy fine cuisine, adult-oriented entertainment, and quieter pools.

Hotels that are environmentally friendly: The Riviera Maya has a number of hotels that are sustainable and environmentally friendly. While providing visitors with a special connection to nature, these residences are built to have little influence on the environment. There are eco-lodges that employ sustainable building materials, run on renewable energy, and offer conservation education.

Luxury Resorts: If you're searching for the height of indulgence, the Riviera Maya is full of them. These hotels frequently provide large rooms, personal butlers, fine dining, and unique experiences. They are ideal for special events or whenever you want to indulge yourself.

3.2 Vacation Rentals

Vacation rentals in the Riviera Maya are a great option for visitors who want more room, solitude, and the chance to blend in with the locals. Families or larger groups will find this option particularly intriguing. What you should know about holiday rentals is as follows:

condominiums and villas: There are several condominiums and villas for rent in the Riviera Maya. These homes frequently have several bedrooms, living areas, and fully functional kitchens. They are ideal for those who want more space to unwind or like to prepare their own meals.

Imagine waking up to the sound of waves breaking on the shore when you rent a beachfront property. In the Riviera Maya, there are lots of beachfront vacation rentals that provide spectacular views and quick access to the sand. For those who want to make the most of their beach time, it's a terrific option.

Private Homes: Private homes in picturesque towns or peaceful neighborhoods are included in some holiday rentals. Staying in a neighborhood where locals live might provide you a more authentic cultural experience because you can explore the region like a native rather than a visitor.

Short-Term Apartments: You can rent a short-term apartment in a comfortable and affordable manner in urban regions like Playa del Carmen or Tulum. These completely furnished residences are frequently close to eateries, shopping, and tourist attractions.

Online Platforms: A variety of online sites, including Airbnb and Vrbo, provide access to a large number of vacation rentals on the Riviera Maya. These systems make it simple to locate, contact, and book property managers or owners.

3.3 Camping and Eco-Lodges

Camping and eco-lodges in the Riviera Maya offer a distinctive experience that enables you to be near to the area's natural beauties for the adventurous and nature-loving traveler. What to anticipate from these choices is as follows:

For those who like to sleep under the stars, the Riviera Maya offers both campgrounds and coastal camping areas. For budget tourists and outdoor enthusiasts, this is a great option. However, be ready for basic amenities and respect the environment by using eco-friendly camping techniques.

Eco-Lodges: The Riviera Maya is renowned for its dedication to sustainability and the protection of the environment. Eco-lodges are created to be environmentally responsible and provide a more complete experience of nature. Bungalows, huts, and treehouses can be found in the forest or by the sea. Eco-lodges frequently use sustainable methods and offer opportunities for you to get in touch with nature through pursuits like birding and guided nature walks, among other things.

Glamping: This trend has gained popularity in the Riviera Maya and combines the comforts of a resort with the outdoorsy feel of camping. While still being near to nature, you can stay in luxurious safari tents or yurts with plush beds, electricity, and private bathrooms. Travelers who want a special balance of luxury and excitement may consider glamping.

You've learned about the several types of lodging available in the Riviera Maya in this part, from the opulent comfort of all-inclusive resorts to the unique adventure of eco-lodges and the adaptability of vacation rentals. With so many options, you may customize your stay to fit your travel preferences and make the most of your trip to this tropical haven. The Riviera Maya's thrilling activities and attractions are covered in detail in the next section of the guide.

EXPLORING THE RIVIERA MAYA

The Riviera Maya is a place of exploration, incredible natural beauty, and a deep cultural history. We'll delve into the wide variety of activities and attractions that are available to you in this alluring location in this part. Everyone can find something to enjoy here, regardless of whether they enjoy the beach, history, wildlife, or extreme sports.

4.1 Beaches and Coastal Activities

Some of the world's most exquisite beaches may be found along the Riviera Maya's breathtaking coastline. Here are some suggestions for coastal pursuits that will help you maximize your time by the water:

Relaxing on the Beaches: The Riviera Maya's beaches are ideal for unwinding, with their beautiful white sands and turquoise waters.

Playa del Carmen, Tulum, and Akumal are a few of the well-known coastal resorts. These beaches provide the perfect location for sunbathing, reading, or taking a leisurely swim.

Snorkeling & diving: With a variety of cenotes (natural sinkholes) and bright coral reefs to discover, the Riviera Maya is a snorkeler and diver's paradise. Snorkelers can dive into the crystal-clear waters of Dos Ojos cenote or swim with sea turtles at Akumal Bay. The Great Maya Reef offers a world of underwater treasures, including vibrant marine life and shipwrecks, for experienced divers.

Water Sports: From paddleboarding and kayaking to kiteboarding and jet-skiing, the area provides a wide variety of water sports. You can learn to windsurf or go on a boat tour with a guide to view the underwater splendor of cenotes and caves.

Visit the eco-parks of Xel-Há and Xcaret, which blend the natural splendor of the outdoors with water pursuits and cultural encounters. While learning about the geography and ecology of the area, you can tour archaeological sites, float down rivers, and snorkel in cenotes.

4.2 Archaeological Sites

Ancient Mayan ruins can be explored on the Riviera Maya, which is rich in history. The following prominent archeological sites provide a peek into the past:

The most famous Mayan ruin in the area is Chichen Itza, a UNESCO World Heritage Site and one of the New Seven Wonders of the World. Investigate the Temple of the Warriors, the Great Ball Court, and the Kukulkan Pyramid.

Tulum: This beautiful archaeological site is perched on a cliff overlooking the Caribbean Sea. The Temple of the Frescoes and El Castillo are two of its well-preserved buildings. A distinctive fusion of history and seaside beauty may be found in Tulum.

Cobá: This jungle-dwelling city is well-known for the enormous Nohoch Mul pyramid, which is the largest structure on the Yucatán Peninsula. For a comprehensive perspective of the surrounding jungle, climb the pyramid.

Muyil: This less well-known location offers a serene setting. For a view of the area's natural splendor, you can see ancient temples and take a boat trip through the Sian Ka'an Biosphere Reserve.

4.3 Natural Parks and Wildlife

The different habitats and plethora of species in the Riviera Maya are a blessing. The following natural areas and wildlife encounters will bring you closer to nature:

The Sian Ka'an Biosphere Reserve is a sizable area of tropical forest, marshes, and coral reefs. It is a UNESCO World Heritage Site. Jaguars, howler monkeys, and a diversity of bird species are among the animals that call it home. Guided tours give you the chance to discover its splendor.

Rio Secreto: At Rio Secreto, explore the Riviera Maya's subterranean rivers. To investigate the underground realm of stalactites and stalagmites, you'll put on a wetsuit, helmet, and headlamp. It's a fascinating and distinctive experience.

Xel-Há Eco-Park: Xel-Há provides spectacular natural landscapes, a refuge for local species, and water experiences. Watch out for the park's amiable parrots, iguanas, and colorful fish.

Akumal: Akumal is well known for the abundance of sea turtles there. These friendly animals frequently come into close proximity to snorkelers as they feed on sea grass in the shallow seas.

4.4 Water Sports and Activities

The Riviera Maya provides a wide range of water sports and activities for people looking for excitement and adventure:

Cenote Diving: Dive into the freshwater sinkholes to discover the region's distinctive cenotes. These submerged caves' stalactites and stalagmites give the area a surreal feel.

Kiteboarding: The Riviera Maya is a hub for kiteboarding due to its reliable winds. Both novice and seasoned kiteboarders can take lessons and rent equipment.

Fishing at depths: The Caribbean Sea is a great place to go deep-sea fishing. Catching marlin, sailfish, and other big game fish is an option.

Cavern and Cave Diving: The Riviera Maya is renowned for its experiences in cavern and cave diving. Divers can experience a special and fascinating environment in these cenotes.

Whale Shark Tours: If you go during the summer, you can go on an unforgettable adventure by swimming with whale sharks. These gentle giants congregate in the waters off Isla Mujeres and Holbox.

You can immerse yourself in a range of experiences as you tour the Riviera Maya, from unwinding on pristine beaches and snorkeling in cenotes to learning about the rich history of Mayan civilisation and touring the region's various ecosystems and animals. A more thorough overview of the Riviera Maya's history and colorful culture will be provided in the following section of this guide.

CULTURE AND HISTORY

The Riviera Maya is a location rich in culture and history in addition to its natural beauty and adventure. This section will take you on a tour of the ancient Mayan legacy, the vivid regional celebrations and traditions, and the museums and cultural institutions that offer a glimpse into the vivacious Riviera Maya culture.

5.1 Mayan Heritage

The ancient Maya civilization, which flourished here for thousands of years, had its center in the Riviera Maya. There are many opportunities to learn more about the region's continued Mayan influence, including:

The famed Chichen Itza, Tulum, Cobá, and Muyil are just a few of the well-preserved Mayan ruins that can be found in the Riviera Maya. Each location provides a look into the Maya's achievements in architecture and culture.

30

Pyramids, temples, and complex carvings that have lasted the test of time can be marveled at.

Sacred Cenotes: For the Mayans, cenotes, or natural sinkholes, had immense spiritual significance. They were regarded as portals into the underworld. These cenotes can now be used for swimming, snorkeling, or diving, giving you a unique viewpoint on Mayan beliefs and practices.

Mayan communities: Getting to know the descendants of the ancient culture is possible by visiting real Mayan communities. You can discover more about their customary way of life, which includes weaving, farming, and cooking. By purchasing handcrafted goods, you can support regional craftsmen.

Traditional Mayan performances, including dance and music, are presented frequently throughout the Riviera Maya's resorts and cultural institutions. These programs offer a glimpse into Mayan storytelling and mythology.

Guided archaeological tours at Mayan sites help visitors gain a greater understanding of the culture. The most recent archaeological findings, stories, and historical context can all be provided by knowledgeable guides.

5.2 Local Festivals and Traditions

Festivals and customs that highlight the Riviera Maya's rich legacy are abundant on the cultural calendar of the region. The following are a some of the most notable holidays and customs:

The Day of the Dead, also known as Dia de los Muertos, is a colorful and significant celebration observed throughout Mexico. You can see altars decked in bright colors, cemeteries with decorations, and parades honoring loved ones who have passed away on the Riviera Maya. The holiday is typically observed from October 31 to November 2.

Holy Week is a religious celebration that is celebrated in the days before Easter. Processions, religious rituals, and regional cuisine can all be found in the Riviera Maya at this time. Both residents and visitors value Semana Santa as an important occasion.

Fiestas de la Virgen de Guadalupe: This celebration honors the Virgin of Guadalupe, the nation of Mexico's patron saint, and is held on December 12. Religious processions, folk dances, and feasts are all part of the festivities. To honor this day, numerous communities in the Riviera Maya host festive celebrations.

Carnaval: Celebrated with vibrant parades, music, dancing, and spectacular costumes, Carnaval occurs just before the start of Lent. The Carnaval celebration in Cozumel, which includes boisterous street celebrations and cultural activities, is particularly well-known.

Festival of Life and Death Traditions at Xcaret: From October 30 to November 2, the eco-archaeological site Xcaret holds its annual Festival of Life and Death Traditions. The celebration features concerts, workshops, and altar exhibitions that highlight Day of the Dead customs.

5.3 Museums and Cultural Centers

Visit one of the following museums or cultural centers to learn more about the history and culture of the Riviera Maya:

The famed Mexican artist Frida Kahlo is honored in this museum, which is located in Playa del Carmen. It includes displays of her artwork, things, and a garden that she designed.

Cancun's Museo Maya: This museum is devoted to the history and civilization of the Mayans. There is an incredible array of tools, pottery, and sculptures available there. Interactive exhibits offer enlightening perspectives on Mayan civilization.

Xcaret Park: Xcaret is a cultural hub in addition to being an ecological park. It sponsors several cultural occasions and displays that examine the history and customs of Mexico. "Xcaret México Espectacular," the park's nighttime performance, is a colorful celebration of Mexican culture.

The Museo de la Cultura Maya in Chetumal explores the history and culture of the Maya people in the area. Chetumal is the state capital of Quintana Roo. There are antiques, works of art, and information on the local indigenous peoples on display.

Tequila and mariachi music are two key facets of Mexican culture that are explored in depth at the Museo de la Tequila y el Mariachi in Playa del Carmen. You can study the origins of these customs and even partake in a tasting.

The history, art, and customs of the Riviera Maya can be studied in further detail at these museums and cultural institutions. There are places to pique your interest in anything from ancient civilizations to modern Mexican art to the distinctive customs of the area.

Travelers may connect with ancient Mayan legacy, take part in exciting regional celebrations, and visit museums that honor Mexico's past and present thanks to the Riviera Maya's rich and diverse culture and history. The gastronomic treats of the area, where you may enjoy the tastes of Mexico and the Riviera Maya, will be the subject of the following portion of this book.

DINING AND CUISINE

The rich history and diverse cultures of the Riviera Maya are reflected in the region's thriving food scene, which is a tapestry of flavors. You can choose from a variety of dining alternatives to satiate your palate, ranging from traditional Mexican food to international fusion cuisine. In this section, we'll look at the regional specialties, top dining establishments, and markets and street cuisine that make up the Riviera Maya's culinary scene.

6.1 Local Foods and Flavors

The food of the Riviera Maya is a delicious fusion of indigenous Mayan flavors, conventional Mexican cuisines, and elements from other cultures. Here are some tasty regional fare to sample:

Ceviche: The Riviera Maya specializes at seafood meals as a coastal area, and ceviche is a popular. For a sour and spicy treat, fresh fish or shrimp are "cooked" in lime juice and combined with cilantro, onions, and occasionally habanero chiles.

Tacos: Tacos are a well-known Mexican delicacy that are available all around the Riviera Maya. Try the traditional Yucatecan delicacy "cochinita pibil," which is made of marinated pork that is slowly roasted, or the neighborhood favorite "pescado" (fish) tacos.

Sikil Pak: Made from pulverized pumpkin seeds, tomatoes, and spices, sikil pak is a classic Mayan dip. It's creamy and nutty and frequently served with tortilla chips.

Mexican cuisine is known for its rich, complicated sauce known as mole. There are several types, such as mole poblano, which uses chocolate, and mole verde, which uses green chilies. Over chicken or turkey, these sauces are frequently used.

Tamales: Popular street food is tamales. They are made of masa (corn dough), which is then filled with various foods like cheese, vegetables, and meats. They are cooked after being wrapped in corn or banana leaves.

Achiote: Made from the seeds of the annatto tree, achiote is a reddish-orange spice. Many regional cuisines, like cochinita pibil, use it to add flavor and color.

Agua Frescas: These hydrating drinks are made from water, sugar, and fresh fruit. Try traditional flavors like tamarind, jamaica (hibiscus), and horchata (rice and cinnamon).

Tequila and Mezcal: Tequila and mezcal are famous throughout Mexico. These alcoholic beverages can be either neat or mixed into drinks like margaritas or palomas. Visit neighborhood bars and restaurants to experience various flavors.

6.2 Restaurants and Dining Options

The Riviera Maya has a wide variety of dining establishments, including both fine dining establishments and fast food joints. Here are some suggestions for each of them:

Fine Dining: If you're searching for a classy dining experience, have a peek at some of the fine dining spots in the area. Gourmet meals are served in unusual settings, such sitting in a natural cave or an Italian patio, at restaurants like "Alux" in Playa del Carmen or "Cenacolo" in Tulum.

Beachfront Dining: A lot of beachfront restaurants provide a lovely environment for a relaxed lunch with a view or a romantic supper. At establishments like "La Zebra" in Tulum, you can sip cocktails and eat fresh fish while dipping your toes in the sand.

Restaurants serving classic Mexican food include "El Fogón" in Playa del Carmen, which is renowned for its delectable tacos al pastor, and "La Cueva del Chango" in the same city, which offers traditional fare in a lovely garden setting.

International Cuisine: The Riviera Maya has restaurants from across the world to suit a variety of tastes. Italian pizzerias and Japanese sushi cafes are among the options. Avoid missing "Hartwood" in Tulum, which is renowned for its wood-fired cuisine made with regional ingredients.

Local street food stands provide a great opportunity to enjoy authentic cuisine at reasonable pricing. Indulge in some churros from a food cart or try a cochinita pibil torta from a street seller.

Visit your local markets and food halls if you're want to sample a wide range of cuisines. A variety of food sellers may be found in locations like "Mercado 28" in Cancun and "El Pueblito" in Mayakoba, providing everything from fresh fruit to local delicacies.

6.3 Street Food and Markets

The Riviera Maya's markets and street food are the best places to sample the region's genuine flavors. What you need know about these gastronomic treasures is as follows:

Taco stalls: Tacos are a common street dish, and taco stalls can be found practically anywhere. A variety of meats and salsas should be tried, and for an extra taste boost, don't forget to add some pickled red onions and habanero sauce.

Elotes and Esquites are traditional corn-based Mexican street dishes. Elotes are corn ears covered in mayo, cheese, chile, lime, and other ingredients, whereas esquites are served in a cup and are therefore more portable.

Churros stands: Churros are fried dough pastries that are frequently sprinkled with cinnamon and sugar to satisfy your sweet craving. They are a well-liked snack in neighborhood markets and food carts.

Fruit Stalls: There are many fresh fruit stands that sell a variety of tropical fruits. Consider exotic alternatives like mamey sapote and pitaya (dragon fruit). Additionally, some sellers make fruit cups with lime juice and chile spice.

Cenote Snack Bars: Snack bars that provide regional treats like empanadas, fresh coconuts, and ceviche are frequently found when exploring cenotes or natural parks.

Markets: For a wide selection of snacks and street cuisine, visit nearby markets. Try local specialties like cochinita pibil or salbutes, which are little fried tortillas topped with meat and vegetables, at Cancun's Mercado 28.

Food Halls: In Mayakoba, food halls like El Pueblito offer a variety of dining options. In one handy location, you may browse kiosks and carts selling regional and international cuisine.

The Riviera Maya's culinary scene is an adventure in food waiting to be discovered, whether you're looking for the best street tacos, hidden gems in the local markets, or fine dining. In this tropical paradise, there is something to please every pallet, from hearty Mayan flavors to global fusions. The lively nightlife and entertainment alternatives that the Riviera Maya has to offer will be covered in more detail in the following section of this guide.

SHOPPING AND SOUVENIRS

You can take a little piece of this tropical paradise home with you if you go shopping in the Riviera Maya. There are many opportunities to find one-of-a-kind items, from artisan markets and souvenir shops to sophisticated boutiques. We'll look at artisan markets, gift shops, and suggested shopping destinations in this section.

7.1 Artisan Markets

The Riviera Maya is renowned for its thriving artisan markets where you can find a huge selection of locally made goods. The following are some of the best artisan marketplaces to visit:

Mercado 28 (Market 28) is a lively market in the heart of Cancun known for its Mexican handicrafts. You can buy pottery, silver jewelry, leather goods, and fabrics with embroidery. Here, haggling over costs is customary, so don't be afraid to do it.

Tulum Art Club: Local artists and craftspeople are featured at this art fair in Tulum. A wide variety of handmade goods, such as paintings, ceramics, textiles, and jewelry, are available. Additionally, the market holds exhibitions and art activities.

Mercado Municipal de Playa del Carmen (Playa del Carmen Municipal Market): In addition to a wide variety of regional crafts and mementos, this market is a fantastic place to buy fresh fruit. Hammocks, embroidered apparel, and authentic Mexican souvenirs are all available.

Pueblito Escondido is a lovely market that honors Mexican workmanship, and it is housed within the opulent Mayakoba complex. It includes one-of-a-kind items from different parts of Mexico, such as handwoven fabrics, ceramics from Oaxaca, and modern art.

7.2 Souvenir Shops

The Riviera Maya has many souvenir shops where you may buy keepsakes from your stay in addition to artist markets. Key mementos to search for include the following:

Mexican Pottery: Many gift shops sell vibrant Mexican pottery, such as talavera and ceramics. These things make wonderful complements to your home's decor because they frequently have complicated patterns and vivid colors.

Hammocks: From the Yucatán Peninsula, hammocks are a common and useful memento. They are ideal for unwinding in your yard or on your balcony because they come in a variety of sizes, hues, and designs.

Textiles: Popular choices for souvenirs include traditional textiles from Mexico. Keep an eye out for embroidered items like garments, tablecloths, or colorful sarapes (blankets).

Lucha Libre Masks: If you're looking for a funny and distinctive souvenir, think about getting a Mexican wrestling (lucha libre) mask. They are a fun addition to your collection and are excellent conversation starters.

Silver jewelry: Mexican silversmithing is known worldwide. There are many different pieces of silver jewelry available, such as rings, necklaces, bracelets, and earrings, many of which have elaborate designs and semiprecious stones.

Tequila and mezcal: Bottles of these spirits are wonderful presents and keepsakes. Choose premium brands, and think about buying straight from regional distilleries.

7.3 Recommended Shopping Areas

The Riviera Maya has a number of retail districts where you may browse boutiques, artisan markets, and gift shops. Here are some areas that are suggested for shopping:

Playa del Carmen's La Quinta Avenida (Fifth Avenue) is a busy pedestrian area that is surrounded by stores, eateries, and bars. In addition to jewelry, apparel, and local handicrafts, it is a great place to look for souvenirs.

Playa del Carmen's Calle Corazón is a fashionable shopping area with upmarket boutiques, art galleries, and department stores. Designer apparel, distinctive jewelry, and modern art can all be found there.

Plaza La Isla, Cancun: This open-air shopping center in Cancun is well-known for its premium boutiques, high-end brands, and a variety of food establishments. It's the ideal location for upscale eating and waterfront shopping.

Playa del Carmen's Paseo del Carmen is a shopping district with a mix of well-known retailers and independent stores next to the Cozumel ferry station. It's a handy location to look around before taking a ferry to the island.

Playa del Carmen's Mayakoba El Pueblito: As previously indicated, this lovely retail district within the Mayakoba complex provides a carefully curated variety of Mexican artisanal goods and one-of-a-kind bargains.

Mercado Ki Huic, Tulum: If you're in Tulum, stop by this laid-back market to buy locally manufactured goods like apparel, jewelry, and home furnishings.

You'll find a variety of stunning and genuine souvenirs that perfectly capture the spirit of this tropical paradise as you browse the marketplaces and retail areas of the Riviera Maya. You'll have a physical memento of your unforgettable visit, whether it's a piece of bright pottery, a hammock that was handmade, or a special item of Mexican jewelry. The Riviera Maya experience will be seamless and delightful thanks to the advice and insights provided in the final portion of this travel book.

NIGHTLIFE AND ENTERTAINMENT

As different as the location itself is the nightlife on the Riviera Maya. The area offers a vibrant and active environment for nighttime entertainment, whether you're looking for lively pubs and clubs, live music and performances, or intriguing events and festivals.

8.1 Bars and Clubs

The vibrant bars and clubs that make up the Riviera Maya's nightlife are legendary. Consider these well-known locations:

Playa del Carmen's Coco Bongo is a renowned nightclub that combines music, acrobatics, and live entertainment. Not to be missed, it's a high-octane, multi-sensory event.

Cancun's Mandala Beach Club offers beachside parties, DJ performances, and poolside dancing.

It is situated in the hotel zone of Cancun. For those looking for a day-to-night experience, it is a favorite.

Playa del Carmen's La Vaquita is a popular nightclub with an eccentric cow-themed interior and a buzzing atmosphere. It's a terrific location for dancing and drinking.

Abolengo, Tulum: Abolengo is a hip rooftop bar with breathtaking ocean views in Tulum. It's a chic location for late-night conversation and cocktails.

Cancun's Palazzo is an opulent nightclub featuring a performance a la Vegas. It provides a variety of music, live acts, and a lavish atmosphere.

Playa del Carmen's Fusion Beach Bar and Grill is a beachfront bar and restaurant ideal for a more leisurely evening. Watch the water while sipping beverages and listening to live music.

8.2 Live Music and Shows

The Riviera Maya features a wide variety of live entertainment options if you desire it:

Live salsa bands can be found in a lot of the pubs and clubs in Playa del Carmen. You can dance to bachata, merengue, and salsa beats. Try the renowned "Alux" cave restaurant in Playa del Carmen for an authentic experience.

A night of music, dance, and Mexican customs is presented at Cancun's Xoximilco cultural park. In trajineras (brightly colored boats), you may take part in a roving fiesta along canals.

Live jazz at the Casa de la Cultura in Playa del Carmen: Live jazz performances are frequently held in the Casa de la Cultura in Playa del Carmen. It's a wonderful location to enjoy outstanding musicians in a cozy setting.

Cultural Shows: The Riviera Maya is home to numerous resorts that put on shows that include Mexican folk dance, music, and storytelling.

Mariachi Bands: At several bars and eateries all across the area, take in the recognizable music of mariachi bands. They frequently integrate classic and traditional Mexican songs in their upbeat concerts.

8.3 Events and Festivals

Throughout the year, the Riviera Maya is the site of numerous festivals and events. Here are some noteworthy examples:

Celebrations on the Day of the Dead (Da de los Muertos) take place from late October to early November. You can see vibrant altars, processions, and celebrations held in memory of loved ones who have passed away.

Jazz musicians from throughout the world and the Playa del Carmen area perform in the Riviera

Maya Jazz Festival, which is typically held in November.

The annual Riviera Maya Film Festival features both Mexican and foreign films. It's a wonderful chance to take in screenings, world premieres, and filmmaker Q&A sessions.

The International Festival of Life and Death Traditions, which takes place at Xcaret Park from late October to early November, honors Mexican Day of the Dead customs via art, music, dance, and theatrical productions.

Winemakers, chefs, and sommeliers from all over the world are featured in the Riviera Maya Wine and Food Festival. For lovers of food and wine, it is a must-see.

Carnaval Cozumel: This dynamic and exuberant celebration, which takes place in February, includes parades, music, dance, and colorful costumes.

BPM Festival: In the past, Playa del Carmen hosted the popular BPM Festival, an electronic music festival, in January. Top DJs from around the world were present. Check out the most recent details on local music festivals.

Whether you want to dance the night away at a vibrant club, enjoy live music and performances, or immerse yourself in regional events and festivals, the nightlife and entertainment options in the Riviera Maya cater to a variety of preferences. It's important to remember that event dates and locations are subject to change, so it's a good idea to check local event listings and venues while you're there to be informed of what's going on.

With the help of this thorough book, you'll be fully equipped to experience the Riviera Maya's natural splendor, culture, gastronomy, and entertainment. This location offers a world of adventures just waiting to be discovered, whether you're planning a leisurely beach vacation or an action-packed excursion.

PRACTICAL INFORMATION

To guarantee a seamless and comfortable travel to the Riviera Maya, it is crucial to have useful information at your fingertips. We'll discuss money and currency exchange, health and safety advice, communication and internet access, as well as what to pack for your trip, in this part.

9.1 Money and Currency Exchange

Mexican Peso (MXN) is Mexico's official currency. It is advised to have extra cash on hand for little transactions and in case you visit locations where credit cards are not accepted.

ATMs: In big towns and cities like Playa del Carmen, Tulum, and Cancun, ATMs are easily accessible. Your debit or credit card can be used to withdraw Mexican Pesos. Keep in mind that some banks may impose foreign transaction fees and unfavorable exchange rates. In order to comprehend the terminology, check with your bank.

Currency Exchange: Tourist hotspots have a ton of exchange offices. To achieve a fair exchange, it's a good idea to compare prices at various locations. Additionally, hotels might provide currency exchange services, but their rates might not be as good.

Credit Cards: Hotels, restaurants, and larger institutions all take credit cards. Both Visa and MasterCard are widely accepted. Although not as common, American Express and Discover are accepted. Cash may be preferred by smaller companies and street vendors.

Tipping: In Mexico, tipping is traditional. A tip of between 10% and 15% is customary at restaurants, but it's wise to check your bill to see if a service fee has already been added. Tipping is also traditional for hotel workers, tour guides, and taxi drivers.

9.2 Health and Safety

Health Caution: Although the Riviera Maya boasts first-rate medical facilities, it is advisable to carry travel insurance that includes medical coverage. Ask your doctor about the necessary vaccines and safety measures before coming to the area.

Water: To avoid any potential gastrointestinal pain, it is advised to drink bottled water. When brushing your teeth, use bottled water and stay away from drinks sold by roadside sellers or small businesses that contain ice.

Sun protection: The Riviera Maya's sun can be very strong. To avoid sunburn and heatstroke, use sunscreen with a high SPF, wear a helmet, and drink enough of water.

Insect repellent: Mosquitoes can be an annoyance in some places, particularly those close to natural cenotes and jungles. To prevent bug bites, use insect repellent.

Travelers can feel somewhat safe visiting the Riviera Maya. But it's a good idea to follow the usual safety precautions. Use hotel safes, lock your valuables, and avoid exhibiting expensive stuff. When swimming in the ocean, exercise caution and follow the recommendations of the lifeguards. Strong currents can be hazardous in some places.

9.3 Communication and Internet Access

cell devices: Ask your cell phone operator about data plans and foreign roaming alternatives. Buying a local SIM card can be cost-effective if you want to remain for a long time or require additional data.

Wi-Fi: The majority of hotels, resorts, and eateries in tourist locations provide access to Wi-Fi. While many places provide free WiFi, some could need a password or your business.

Communication applications: To avoid paying roaming fees when traveling, think about using communication applications like WhatsApp, Skype, or FaceTime if you need to make international calls or communicate with others.

9.4 Packing and What to Bring

The season and your intended activities will determine what to pack for your trip to the Riviera Maya. Here are some necessities to think about:

Pack breathable, light-weight clothing that is appropriate for warm temperatures. Don't forget your swimsuits, casual clothing for going out to eat, and comfortable walking shoes.

Sun protection: To shield oneself from the harsh sun, you should wear sunscreen, sunglasses, and a wide-brimmed hat.

Bring insect repellant to fend off mosquitoes and other bugs, especially if you intend to visit nature regions.

Medication: Make sure you have a sufficient supply if you need specialized medications or have allergies.

Electronics: Don't forget to bring any essential power converters, chargers, and electrical equipment. Additionally useful are a power bank or portable charger.

Passport, visa, travel insurance, and any other necessary travel documents should be kept in a safe location. Create copies or electronic backups.

Carrying local money is advised for modest purchases and locations that don't take credit cards.

A tiny day bag or backpack is helpful for carrying the necessities for day travels.

Reusable water bottles are a sustainable way to remain hydrated and cut down on plastic waste.

Reusable Shopping Bag: Since some communities have begun to restrict single-use plastic bags, carrying one around with you when you shop can be useful.

Bring travel-sized items with you, such as soap, shampoo, and a toothbrush. Although many hotels offer these amenities, it's always a good idea to have your favorite brands on hand.

Having a phrasebook or translation app can be useful for talking in Spanish, even if many inhabitants in tourist locations understand a little English.

Adventure Gear: Don't forget your swimsuit, snorkel gear, water shoes, and the suitable attire for the activity if you intend to explore cenotes, go snorkeling, or engage in outdoor adventures.

There's no need to bring formal dress because the Riviera Maya offers a laid-back, beachy attitude. To ensure a pleasurable and hassle-free time in this tropical paradise, choose cozy apparel and useful items.

With these helpful hints, you'll be equipped to enjoy your trip to the Riviera Maya to the fullest. This location provides a universe of activities just waiting to be discovered, whether you're unwinding on the stunning beaches, discovering the historic Mayan ruins, enjoying regional cuisine, or getting lost in the exciting nightlife.

CHRISTMAS IN THE RIVIERA MAYA

The Rivièra Maya provides a distinctive and wonderful setting for Christmas celebrations with its beautiful beaches, pleasant climate, and rich cultural legacy. You'll find a variety of festive customs, seasonal activities, and unique dining and entertainment alternatives to make your Christmas a genuinely unforgettable experience if you're going to spend the holiday season in this tropical paradise.

10.1 Festive Traditions and Celebrations

Christmas in the Riviera Maya may not have the typical wintry scenery associated with the holiday, but it more than makes up for it with its own distinctive customs and festivities. Here are a few ways the area celebrates Christmas:

Nativity Scenes: "nacimientos," or nativity scenes, are a significant component of Mexican

Christmas customs. These elaborate displays can be seen in people's homes, churches, and public spaces. Even life-sized nativity scenes with actors and live animals are created in some localities.

Las Posadas: "Las Posadas" depicts Mary and Joseph looking for a place to stay in Bethlehem. Processions, carol singing, and breaking piatas are all part of this custom. In the Riviera Maya, a lot of hotels and resorts have their own Las Posadas for visitors to enjoy.

Christmas Eve: In Mexico, the holiday season's major attraction is frequently Christmas Eve (Nochebuena). Families get together for a joyful lunch that frequently includes classic delicacies like tamales, ponche, and salted cod (bacalao). Christmas Eve festivities frequently include fireworks and gatherings in public spaces.

Misa de Gallo: In the days preceding Christmas, a special early-morning church service known as "Misa de Gallo" or "Rooster's Mass" is held. It's a major custom in Mexico that symbolizes the countdown to Jesus' birth.

Christmas is celebrated with elaborate firework displays, especially on Christmas Eve. In the Riviera Maya, numerous towns and communities light up the night sky with brilliant fireworks. In addition, beautiful holiday light displays can be found in busy places.

Tizimn's Feria de la Piata is a fun festival that you should check out if you're in the neighborhood. Tizimn is a picturesque village on the Yucatán Peninsula. In the weeks before Christmas, this celebration hosts parades, cultural events, and colorful piatas.

10.2 Holiday Events and Activities

When it comes to seasonal activities and events that cater to travelers hoping to get into the Christmas spirit, the Riviera Maya doesn't fall short. The following are some fun holiday choices to consider:

Christmas markets: Known as "tianguis navideos," these markets are open during the holiday season and are a great place to find handmade goods, seasonal decorations, and gifts. Live entertainment and music can frequently be found at these markets.

Festival of Light and Sound at Xcaret: During the Christmas season, the eco-archaeological site Xcaret holds a Festival of Light and Sound. This spectacular occasion mixes music, dancing, and light shows to highlight Mexico's rich cultural and ecological heritage.

Playa del Carmen's Pueblito de los Reyes: During the holiday season, this charming market comes to life. With decorations, music, and a variety of vendors selling holiday-themed goods, it has a joyful environment.

Christmas at Xoximilco Park: The cultural park in Cancun, Xoximilco, celebrates the season with unique trajinera (boat) rides that are styled in the style of Christmas. Live music, a festive ambiance, and authentic Mexican food are available.

Christmas Eve Dinners: There are numerous hotels and resorts on the Riviera Maya that serve festive meals on Christmas Eve. These elaborate feasts make for a spectacular holiday eating experience because they frequently feature both traditional Mexican food and cuisine from other countries.

Holiday Concerts and Shows: Keep an eye out for concerts and shows with a holiday theme at nearby theaters, museums, and resorts. You may watch a range of live performances, including choirs and mariachi bands.

Holiday Celebrations at Resorts: If you're visiting the Riviera Maya and staying at a resort, you'll probably discover a variety of holiday activities and festivities planned by the resort. Watch for special Christmas-themed banquets, performances, and decorations.

10.3 Special Dining and Entertainment

The Riviera Maya offers special eating and entertainment opportunities for Christmas celebrations. Here are some locations and choices to take into account for a unique Christmas celebration:

Christmas Dinners at Local Restaurants: The Riviera Maya is home to a large number of eateries, particularly those in popular tourist locations. These establishments offer unique Christmas dinners with a range of culinary selections, including both Mexican and international cuisine.

Resort Celebrations: Resorts in the area go above and beyond to make their visitors' Christmases special. Families may anticipate opulent meals, holiday decorations, live entertainment, and even visits from Santa Claus.

Consider having Christmas dinner at a restaurant with ocean views that is beachside. The sound of the waves combined with a beautiful sunset creates a magical atmosphere for the vacation.

Dinner Cruises: Along the coast, some operators offer special Christmas dinner cruises. A special way to mark the occasion is with a meal for two under the stars.

Private Celebrations: If you're traveling in a group or with a family, you may be able to have a special Christmas celebration with your loved ones at one of the resorts or restaurants that provide private dining options.

Nightclubs and bars: Some nightclubs and bars organize Christmas parties with DJs, dancing, and seasonal drinks for people who prefer a livelier and more out-of-the-ordinary celebration.

Christmas on the Riviera Maya offers a singular opportunity to combine your own customs with the voluminous and vivacious Mexican festivities. The Riviera Maya offers a warm and inviting atmosphere for spending Christmas, whether you're attending a traditional Posada, taking in a holiday meal, or visiting the seasonal markets. Make the most of your vacation in this tropical paradise by embracing the holiday spirit.

ADDITIONAL RESOURCES

As you plan your trip to the Riviera Maya, it's important to have access to useful resources to enhance your travel experience. Here, we'll provide information on websites and apps, local tour operators and services, and essential emergency contacts.

11.1 Useful Websites and Apps

Visit Mexico (Website: visitmexico.com): This official website offers a wealth of information on travel destinations in Mexico, including the Riviera Maya. You can find details on attractions, accommodations, and events.

TripAdvisor (Website and App: tripadvisor.com): TripAdvisor is a valuable resource for traveler reviews, recommendations, and tips. It's a great place to read reviews and get insights from fellow travelers.

XE Currency Converter (App: xe.com): This app provides real-time exchange rates and currency conversion, which can be handy for currency exchange and budgeting.

Google Maps (App: maps.google.com): Google Maps is a reliable tool for navigating the Riviera Maya, offering directions, maps, and local business listings. You can use it to find points of interest, restaurants, and more.

Weather Apps: Various weather apps can help you stay updated on local weather conditions. Some popular choices include Weather.com, AccuWeather, or The Weather Channel app.

Airbnb (Website and App: airbnb.com): If you're considering vacation rentals, Airbnb is a platform to explore accommodations beyond traditional hotels and resorts.

11.2 Local Tour Operators and Services

Amstar DMC (Website: amstardmc.com): Amstar DMC is a reputable tour operator in the Riviera Maya that offers a range of excursions, transportation services, and airport transfers.

Xcaret Group (Website: grupoxcaret.com): Xcaret Group operates eco-archaeological parks in the region, including Xcaret and Xel-Há, which offer a variety of cultural and natural activities.

TUI (Website: tui.com): TUI is a well-known travel company that provides vacation packages, tours, and excursions in the Riviera Maya.

Lomas Travel (Website: lomas-travel.com): Lomas Travel is a local tour operator offering airport transfers, day trips, and tours to popular attractions.

Local Diving and Watersports Centers: If you're interested in diving, snorkeling, or water sports, there are numerous local operators and dive shops in towns like Playa del Carmen and Tulum.

11.3 Emergency Contacts

While the Riviera Maya is generally safe for travelers, it's important to be aware of emergency contacts in case you encounter any unforeseen situations:

Emergency Services: For police, medical, or fire emergencies, dial 911, which is a universal emergency number in Mexico.

Local Police: In case of non-emergency situations or for general inquiries, you can contact the local police at 060.

Tourist Assistance Hotline: For assistance and information specifically for tourists, you can call the Tourist Assistance Hotline at +52 800 903 9200.

Embassies and Consulates: If you're traveling as a foreign national, be aware of the location and contact information for your country's embassy or consulate in Mexico. They can provide assistance with passport issues, legal matters, or other consular services.

CONCLUSION AND FINAL THOUGHTS

The Riviera Maya is a destination that captivates the hearts of travelers with its stunning beaches, rich cultural heritage, and vibrant traditions. This travel guide has offered a comprehensive overview of the region, covering topics from travel tips and transportation to exploring the natural wonders, cultural treasures, and lively nightlife of this tropical paradise.

As you embark on your journey to the Riviera Maya, remember that this region offers a perfect blend of relaxation and adventure. You can bask in the beauty of pristine beaches, snorkel in crystal-clear cenotes, and explore ancient Mayan ruins. At the same time, you'll have the opportunity to immerse yourself in the local culture, savor authentic Mexican cuisine, and partake in exciting holiday celebrations.

With the wealth of activities, delicious flavors, and unforgettable experiences awaiting you, the Riviera Maya promises a memorable and enchanting trip. Whether you're seeking a tranquil beach escape, an exploration of ancient history, or an unforgettable Christmas celebration, this destination provides a diverse range of experiences for all types of travelers.

As you prepare for your trip, don't forget to check the most up-to-date travel advisories, review the latest information on attractions and events, and make necessary reservations. While the information provided in this guide offers a solid foundation, the landscape of travel is ever-changing, so staying informed is key to a smooth and enjoyable visit.

Above all, approach your journey with an open heart and an adventurous spirit, ready to embrace the beauty, culture, and warmth of the Riviera Maya. Whether you're walking along the pristine shores of Tulum, exploring the ancient city of Chichen Itza, or celebrating Christmas with the locals, the memories you create in this tropical paradise will remain with you for a lifetime. Safe travels and enjoy your time in the Riviera Maya!

Printed in Great Britain
by Amazon

37297442R00046